WHY DID GOD MAKE BUGS & OTHER ICKY THINGS

?

Questions Kids Ask

Kel Groseclose

DIMENSIONS
FOR LIVING
NASHVILLE

WHY DID GOD MAKE BUGS AND OTHER ICKY THINGS?



*This book is printed on acid-free, recycled paper.*

**Library of Congress Cataloging-in-Publication Data**

Groseclose, Kel, 1940–
Why did God make bugs and other icky things? : questions kids ask / Kel Groseclose.
p. cm.
ISBN 0-687-46583-4 (alk. paper)
1. Children—Religious life—Miscellanea. I. Title.
BV4571.2.G75 1992
248.8'2—dc20 92-3670
CIP



MANUFACTURED IN THE UNITED STATES OF AMERICA

To John, Steve, Aimee,
Mike, Sara, and Dave

Children who asked me
the hardest questions of all,
and for whom I'm eternally
grateful

# CONTENTS

# INTRODUCTION

Once upon a time there was a child who asked an endless succession of questions. Her father seldom seemed to hear the child. If, by chance, an inquiry made it as far as his ears, he immediately deflected it. "Ask your mother." "Can't you see I'm busy right now?" "That was a dumb question."

One day the child, in a courageous moment, asked her father if he minded being asked so many questions. "Oh, not at all, daughter," he replied with a straight face. "How else will you ever learn anything?"

Children and adults do not always need answers, at least not those of a final, ultimate nature. What they do want is to be heard, to be taken seriously. Children, in particular, need the significant people in their lives to join their quest for knowledge, to be partners in their search for truth, and to walk with them in their struggle for faith.

All of us could benefit from periodic reminders that questioning is not only permissible but highly desirable. It never indicates a lack of faith. Quite the contrary, questioning is one essential mark of a serious seeker. The ability to ask perceptive questions is not a bother but a rare gift.

Frequent inquiries ought not to be the exclusive province of four- and five-year-olds. Questioning is intended to be a lifelong endeavor. Those who stop wondering stop growing. Questions, of course, often have unsettling effects. Head scratching and fingernail biting usually accompany the toughest ones.

Asking questions helps our faith stay fresh and vital. It's a spiritual discipline designed to keep us open to the surprising, creative presence of God.

A hand-me-down system of beliefs will never quite fit, nor will it be fashionable or durable. Each generation must ask the hard questions, challenge the status quo, and strive to find its own unique expressions of faith. Questioning is not the sign of a rebellious child or a meddlesome adult. It is to be valued as an attempt to energize faith and present it winsomely to a waiting world.

From childhood on, Jesus was a questioner of note. Following the infancy accounts, we next hear of him in the Temple listening to the rabbis and asking them questions; some, no doubt, of the knotty, thorny variety. Questioning became a frequent teaching technique in his ministry. In the eighth chapter of Mark's Gospel, Jesus is recorded asking fifteen questions, each one direct and discerning, and culminating in the famous query, "Who do you say that I am?"

Children ask the usual questions relating to daily life. "Do I have to eat my broccoli?" "Why can't I stay up and watch the late movie?" "How come none of my friends has to do as many chores as I do?" The list could and frequently does go on at length.

Do not be put off by these superficialities. Children are also deep thinkers and ask penetrating questions. The parent who has never squirmed uncomfortably from a child's questions is a parent who isn't listening.

Young persons do not really want parents and other adults to act as though they have answers for everything. Rather than stumble through a response that everyone knows is mostly fluff or filler, it is better to frankly admit one's ignorance. At times, the best that can be said is, "I don't know; let's see if we can find the answer together." In our pilgrimage for wisdom, two indispensable qualities are humor and humility.

One hopes the reader has concluded by now that this book's purpose is not so much to provide answers as to celebrate the questions. While finding solutions is satisfying, the process of asking is basic and can be wonderfully exciting in itself.

I promise no easy answers. I pledge only to grapple honestly with questions children are asking, many of which have been debated through the centuries and will likely continue to be debated for years to come. Expect to have even more questions by the last page than you have now at the beginning.

I am grateful to the staff at the Wenatchee First United Methodist Church for their insights, encouragement, and patience; to my spouse, Ellen, for her constant support and for bringing me back when I teetered on the brink of panic; to those parents who graciously offered their encouragement; and to a special group of children for sharing their incisive questions—Lindsey Burke, Josh and Cody Harmening, Andy and Kate Largent, Piper and Laurie McCormack. They made me squirm. The final product, therefore, may be worth reading.

*Kel Groseclose*
*Wenatchee, Washington*
*1991*

# —1—

## WAS JESUS A BABY JUST LIKE ME?

Four-year-old John was looking in his baby album at pictures showing him with spaghetti smeared all over his face; capturing his first wobbly steps; recording his proud grin with two tiny bottom teeth gleaming. It was shortly after Christmas and the birth of Jesus still burned vividly in his memory. Without any warning, as is often the case with children's questions, he asked his mother, "Was Jesus a baby just like me?"

John asked an age-old question. Was Jesus fully human or was God only masquerading as a person? Church leaders of the fourth century addressed this issue at the Council of Nicaea. Of course they used bigger words and more complex sentence structure. They put as many paradoxical concepts as possible in a two-hundred-word creed. After considerable debate and much theological nit-picking, they concluded that, "We believe in one Lord, Jesus Christ, the only Son of God, eternally begotten of the Father, . . . true God from true God. . . . he came down from heaven, was incarnate of the Holy Spirit and the Virgin Mary and became truly human. . . ."

Most of us average folks don't need the entire complicated explanation. A simple yes would suffice. Yes, John, Jesus was a baby just like you. Like every other unborn child, he kicked his mother's tummy as he moved in her womb. We know it happened at least once when Mary was visiting her cousin Elizabeth. Shortly after his birth, he was probably fussy sometimes during the arduous journey to Egypt.

The baby Jesus was dependent on others in the same way newborns are today. He had to be fed and burped, have his diapers (or the first-century equivalent) changed, have his fingernails trimmed, be bathed, and be picked up when he fell down. No doubt he cried when he was hungry and was cranky when cutting teeth.

The security of being held and rocked by Mary and Joseph may have served as the inspiration later in life to encourage little children to come to him. Perhaps playing with childhood friends on Galilean hillsides provided rudimentary skills he would develop in calling and leading the twelve disciples. As he fulfilled his household duties and was a faithful, obedient son, a youthful Jesus surely clarified what would become the focus of his ministry—servanthood in the world.

As an adult, Jesus was very human. He enjoyed eating meals with his followers; cried when those he loved were hurt or sad; became angry when people did unloving things; took pity on crowds of bewildered and hungry people; told jokes, laughed, and sang. He enjoyed the beach, going fishing, visiting with friends, and early morning walks in gardens.

John, when you were born no wise persons came on camels to bring you expensive gifts, did thcy? Shepherds didn't leave their sheep to see what you looked like and pay you homage. Of course, the hospital would likely have refused them entry, reeking as they did of campfire smoke. No bright star shown over the delivery room where you took your first breath. Even so, John, your birth was a miracle! You are special in the sight of God.

Being human isn't always easy. God knows because God's son was a baby just like you. You'll have disappointments, failures, and griefs. But having a God who knows exactly how you feel makes being human a wonderful adventure.

So, my young friend John, keep going forward. Your life's journey is filled with promise.

## —2—

# WHY DID GOD MAKE BUGS AND OTHER ICKY THINGS?

I was working in the garden when a neighbor boy wandered by. "Whatchadoin', Mister?"

"I'm spraying the cabbage."

"How come?"

"To get rid of the bugs."

"How come?"

"Because they eat the plants."

"What for?"

"Because they're hungry." I picked a leaf that had so many holes it resembled a green lace doily.

"Wow! They eat a lot, don't they." There was a pause during which you could almost hear the wheels turning in his young brain. "Mister, did God make bugs and other icky things?"

"Yes, I suppose so. God made everything."

"Well, I think that was a dumb thing for God to do." Satisfied with his conclusion, he went to the sprinkler and ran through it several times. When he was gone, his question lingered in my mind. Why *did* God make bugs and other icky creatures? And why so many? A few we could handle. But they descend upon us in hordes, swarms, and infestations.

When the Creator surveyed creation and pronounced it good, is it possible that insects, snakes, and other creeping, crawling things weren't yet invented? Could it be that at the very beginning, God didn't realize the havoc insects would wreak on humanity? Probably not. So why didn't Noah and his family leave locusts, ticks, mosquitoes, cockroaches, flies, rats, leeches, rattlesnakes, and other troublesome critters behind? But no, Mr.

and Mrs. Noah didn't miss one. Male and female, they escorted a pair of every living creature on board.

Maybe God views these matters differently than we humans do. We define beauty in rather narrow, self-serving terms. If something outwardly pleases us, we consider it attractive. But should a person or animal fail even slightly to meet the established norm, we frequently apply the label "ugly." In any case, the frightening appearance of certain insects and animals may be simply a warning system for humans to keep their distance.

There is order and interdependence among all living things. In our limited understanding, we may not fully realize how everything fits in God's grand scheme. The measure of any living thing's value cannot be determined solely by our human likes or dislikes, by its contribution to the Gross National Product, or by its usefulness for our own purposes. Even the tiniest and the most repulsive forms of life have intrinsic worth. Birds and anteaters no doubt appreciate God's creation of insects.

The answer to this question may be that we need to change our attitudes and refrain from categorizing plants as either weeds or flowers; from dividing insects into beautiful or icky; from classifying people as handsome or homely, friend or foe.

If we were able to communicate with these "lower forms of life," we might discover that they aren't particularly pleased about having to share this planet with us. They may consider us—who litter, pollute, and destroy their habitat—the truly unattractive ones.

In the meantime, if I'm going to have any of my favorite coleslaw, something has to be done about those pesky bugs. I don't begrudge them a place in the sun. I just wish they'd eat lunch in somebody else's cabbage patch.

## —3—

# DO CATS GO TO HEAVEN?

Our house is filled with animals—two dogs and four cats to be exact. At various times, we've hosted hamsters, gerbils, parakeets, tropical fish, guinea pigs, and an orphaned duck who was kept in a cardboard refrigerator box in our living room. When our felines and canines shed, which seems to be all the time, there's a contrasting color of fur for every pair of pants I own.

Pets require a lot of work, but they also bring a great deal of joy. We've come to know each animal's personality—where it likes to be scratched, its eating habits, whether it's playful or serious, and which of my favorite chairs it chooses for a nap. With six pets, sometimes there isn't a comfortable chair left for us humans. The animals are stretched out on cushions, and we're sprawled on the floor.

Having built such deep and lasting bonds, it's natural for children to ask what happens when pets die. Do they go to heaven? Or as one girl inquired, "Do they have their very own heaven?" Another child experienced the loss of both her grandfather and her favorite pet within days of each other. She expressed her wonder in concrete terms. "Did Pasha go to heaven with Grandpa?"

The best response to questions such as this that have no definitive answers is to honestly share one's own feelings. "I loved Pasha just as you did; and if the decision were mine, she'd be curled up at Grandpa's feet right now."

Jesus told the disciples, "About that day or hour no one knows" (Mark 13:32 NRSV). We do not have sufficient information to make official pronouncements concerning eternity. Yet, there's no harm in speculating, as long as we remain humble and draw from what we already know about God's nature.

Personally, I think heaven would be rather bland and boring if life in all its varieties weren't present. Every earthly expression of life is sacred to the Creator. We know that not even a tiny sparrow falls from the sky without God's awareness. God's love reaches out to the lost sheep. God picks up and holds the little lambs. It seems logical and fair that cats and dogs, goldfish and horses should have a place somewhere in everlasting life.

God, who yearns for us to be caring and kind toward all living creatures, also feels compassion for them. The God who makes baby animals so appealing and pets so loyal and faithful, surely has a warm spot for each and every one.

When Ralph the hamster died of natural causes, we put his body in a small shoe box lined with tissue paper. After a few words of remembrance and appreciation, we tenderly buried him beside the backyard peach tree. A large rock served as his headstone. We all cried, especially Michael, who was Ralph's special buddy.

It's comforting to think that maybe Ralph and the other pets I've loved through the years—Trixie, Nugget, Eve, and Henry—will greet me when I enter that life which is eternal. It makes the anticipation of heaven even sweeter.

## —4—

# DOES GOD LOVE ME WHEN I MESS UP?

My father, the preacher, was in the middle of his sermon and about to make a major point. Meanwhile, his loving, obedient son was crouched behind the back pew, messing around as usual. As a small child, I always sat next to my mother in the second row, directly in front of the pulpit. Both parents could keep a close watch on me from that vantage point. As I grew older, however, I was granted the privilege of sitting with friends at the back of the sanctuary. I knew that if I abused the privilege, I might well find myself sitting front and center again.

I wasn't a mean-spirited child. I will admit to being active and mischievous, but not bad. I did the usual pranks like scribbling mustaches and scars on bulletin-cover faces. The apostle Paul, John Wesley, and Martin Luther were frequent recipients of my artistic endeavors. I passed notes back and forth to friends, whispered too loudly during silent meditation, crunched sugar cubes from the church kitchen, and made a variety of paper airplanes, some capable of flying all the way from the balcony to the altar.

But the year I was ten, I really did it. I meant no harm. It was supposed to be a scientific experiment, as I explained later. Yes, I was old enough to know better. A three-year-old would have known better. I just wanted to see what would happen when a lighted match and the corner of the bulletin came close together. I found out in a hurry!

Bulletins, or maybe the mimeograph ink on them, burn exceedingly well. I dropped the paper to the floor and began vigorously stomping on it. It refused to go out. A column of black smoke silently rose from behind the pew.

As the flames finally subsided, I suddenly became aware of a deadly quiet in the place. Peering over the pew, I noticed that my father had ceased preaching and was looking in my direction with a not-too-pleasant look. Most members of the congregation were craning their necks to see what the problem was, their noses twitching from the strong smell of smoke. For some strange reason, people didn't act surprised when they saw that it was the preacher's kid.

I don't remember the rest of the sermon that day. I don't imagine my father did, either. Sunday afternoon dinner was a bit tense for all of us; except for my older sister, who sat there with a holier-than-thou smirk on her face. If it would have helped, I'd have tattled on her about some of the rotten things I'd seen her do. But I figured that with my luck, I'd only get into deeper trouble; and she'd be mad at me as well.

So, it was the pew in the second row for me again, spending several months' worth of worship under the watchful eyes of my mother. It was a small price to pay for my indiscretion. Actually, there were several positive by-products. I improved my listening skills; I learned to love the hymnal from hours of thumbing through it; and I discovered that though my mother sang sharp, she was really quite a wonderful person.

I do remember wondering what God thought about my little shenanigan. Was God disappointed with me? Or did God get a good chuckle over the antics of a lively, energetic boy?

Children sometimes ponder how God can love them constantly and unconditionally when they, like all humans, make frequent mistakes, say hurtful things, and often leave messes behind them. They may question whether God loves them when they get angry, impatient, cranky, or mean.

The answer is an emphatic "yes!" God loves them when they sass their parents, fight with a brother or sister, say naughty words, tell lies, or disobey family rules. God is love through and through.

God's love, however, should not be mistaken for approval. There's a difference between being divinely accepted as a person and having one's actions divinely endorsed. God may not like what we do, but God will never reject who we are. Jesus demonstrated the way of loving without reservations, with no conditions, exclusions, or limitations. Paul expressed it beautifully in

Romans 8:39, "[nothing] in all creation, will be able to separate us from the love of God in Christ Jesus our Lord" (NRSV).

People, including parents, sometimes withhold love when others fail to meet their expectations or hurt their feelings. But to deny kind words, rebuff a gentle touch, or refuse any loving expression are always counterproductive. Such actions usually produce anxiety, rebelliousness, and the very behaviors we're trying to avoid.

I doubt that few children have been nagged into developing more thoughtful, sweeter personalities; or have performed good works joyfully as a result of being bawled out. No one has ever been successfully scolded into receiving the gift of salvation. We are lured into the Reign of God. God prefers to hug, tickle, and giggle us into abundant, eternal life.

God hangs in there with us through tough times and in difficult moments. When we're tempted to do less than our best, God nudges and inspires us to reach for greater things. God's unconditional love is exactly what it's advertised as being—no catches, fine print, or restrictions. Since I continue to mess up on a fairly regular basis, that is comfort indeed!

# —5—

## WHAT WILL JESUS LOOK LIKE WHEN HE COMES BACK TO EARTH?

By the time roll was taken, they were already into the discussion hot and heavy. "I've heard that when things in the world really get terrible, God's going to send Jesus back to wipe out all the bad people."

"I don't believe that," replied Andy, a seventh grader in Mr. Largent's junior high church school class. "If so, why did God send Jesus the way he did the first time?"

"What do you mean?" Kate asked.

"Well, two thousand years ago Jesus was born in a manger, in a little out-of-the-way town, and in a tiny country. His parents were just average folks, nothing special. When it happened, only a few people figured out what was going on. God came to earth quietly; you know, low-key. Why would God cause a commotion and be destructive in the Second Coming?"

"Because not enough people paid attention before."

"Maybe so, but I doubt it. I don't think God's changed."

"Hey, do you suppose they could get Arnold Schwarzeneggar to play the lead?" chimed in another youth. "Or how about Sylvester Stallone?" A girl who'd been silently observing spoke up.

"I don't see why God would send Jesus back to earth at all. If you remember, the first coming didn't end very well. Why would Jesus want to return and go through more suffering?"

"To help us better understand what God wants us to do," Kate replied.

"Could be, but it's not like we're all alone. We already have the Bible to teach us those things. And God's Spirit is always present to guide us in the way we should go."

"Yeh, but it would sure help me if God would wrap up his love and truth again in a flesh-and-blood person."

The same question these youth are wrestling with arose almost immediately following the death of Jesus. The first disciples anticipated his return in their own lifetime and often wondered why it hadn't yet occurred. It's been repeatedly asked down through the ages. At various times in world history, people have believed Jesus' return was imminent. We now seem to be in another such period. When turmoil and tribulation are at high levels, as they are in the late twentieth century, hopes in the Christian community for Jesus' return tend to increase.

The decision and timing of the Second Coming, naturally, are up to God. Chances are good, however, that Jesus will not come to a racially pure, socially proper, upper middle-class town in the United States. We'd be wise to watch for his return in a Third World nation, to an impoverished family in the inner city, or to a young unmarried couple in an obscure Asian village.

It's most unlikely he'll come back as the CEO of a major corporation, a television evangelist, famous movie star, or in any other politically powerful or prominent role. There'll be no Madison Avenue image, no high pressure sales pitch, no Cecil B. deMille Hollywood production number, no hype. God respected our freedom of choice the first time and will no doubt act in the same manner when Jesus comes again.

What Jesus might look like outwardly is far less important than who he will be inwardly. As in his first coming, his appearance will be secondary to his words and deeds. I'm convinced that God does not want us to be overly concerned about Jesus' possible return, and he certainly does not want us to worry about being left out when it does happen. If we love and serve others and seek to fulfill our ministry day by day, we need not lose sleep over this question.

It's good for children and adults to clarify what they believe about it. But we can trust God, who without our input, knew what to do the first time around; and most assuredly, already has an idea or two about how it should take place the next time.

## —6—

# DOES GOD CRY WHEN I GET HURT?

Okay, so Sam's aim wasn't very good. He was only six years old, after all, and hadn't had much experience swinging a hatchet. His family's winter heating supply of mill ends had just been dumped in the driveway. He carefully selected several choice pieces with no knots and was soon busy creating a variety of boats. They were his favorites. When the tugboats, ferries, ocean liners, and battleships were in the bathtub, there was hardly room for Sam. Though the years have gone by, he can still smell the pungent odor of wet ponderosa pine in that warm bathroom.

Sam took a short sabbatical from building while his thumb healed. His mother cleaned the wound and put a bandage over it. That helped assuage the pain. He was comforted even more by the fact that when she saw his tears, she cried, too. It still hurt. He has an inch-long scar on his thumb as a result of his youthful indiscretion. To know that another person felt his pain and was willing to freely enter into it, soothed Sam's whole being. This could explain why a parent's kiss on a child's "ouchie" has instant healing properties.

If we human parents know how to empathize with our children's sorrows and enter into their pain, how much more does our divine Parent know how? God may not shed tears as we do; but God profoundly cares. God weeps over the great injustices and global tragedies, as well as over the small hurts that daily happen to individuals. In addition, the Creator has a delightful sense of humor and joins us in laughter when happy, funny things occur.

God cries when entire societies are denied freedom and equality. God anguishes when races of people are victims of prejudice and hatred. God hurts for the poor, for the refugee and the homeless, for those who are neglected and abused. Yet God still has time to notice and feel the pain from a sliver in a child's finger; from the sting of a scraped knee; the throbbing of a smashed fingernail; and even the shock of a hatchet crunching a thumb.

We read in Scripture that God's Son, Jesus, wept when those he loved suffered. The Spirit of God is close to us; an intimate presence in our lives. God cares so deeply about the welfare of all life that each of our feelings is felt by the heart of God; every experience of ours is incorporated into the mind of God.

When children ask "Does God cry when I get hurt?" or other similarly worded questions, they are seeking assurance that God truly cares for them. They want to know that God is not an absentee landlord who, following creation, left on permanent vacation. They want to experience God as Emmanuel, "God with us."

In a very real sense, the hugs and kisses we share with one another are extensions of God's love. The tears of parents and guardians are concrete expressions of divine compassion for the children of the world. Offering them in liberal dosages is a vital dimension of our Christian faith.

I was privileged to have a mother-in-law who had a seemingly boundless supply of compassion. She loved all her children and grandchildren equally. She accepted her in-laws as though they had been in the family since birth. When any of these were hurting, ill, or having difficulties, Grandma's love went out to that person with an intensity you could almost see. I'm absolutely certain that the healing process was speeded immeasurably by her compassion. You were surrounded, undergirded, and lifted by a love so strong that you immediately improved. There were compelling reasons to keep going. Grandma loved you! She needed you!

Grandma must have gotten that quality somewhere. Actually, I believe she got it from Someone; that same Someone who enters our lives without reservation or condition; who rejoices when we rejoice, who weeps when we weep.

Isn't that a source of wonderful comfort for children of all ages?

# —7—

# WHY CAN'T EVERYBODY JUST LIVE IN PEACE?

"Did too!"
"Did not!"
"Did too!"
"Did not!"
"Boys, that's enough," interrupted Mrs. Mitchell, the third grade teacher at Lewis and Clark School.
"He started it."
"No, I didn't. You did."
"Did not!"
"Did too!"
"I don't care who started it. I want it stopped right now! Is that clear?"
"Yes, Mrs. Mitchell," they replied in unison. If Mrs. Mitchell remembered correctly, this was the sixth shouting and shoving match at recess that week. And it was only Tuesday. A big sigh escaped from her mouth. When the students reassembled in the classroom, acting on a sudden inspiration, she gave them a written assignment. She printed on the chalkboard the following questions: "Why do kids fight so often? Why can't everybody just live in peace?"

After the usual moaning and groaning, the children settled down to work. That evening, in her slippers and robe, and with a cup of her favorite lemon tea, Mrs. Mitchell read their responses. She was pleasantly surprised by their candid and insightful answers.

"Kids fight for the same reasons adults fight—jealousy, hatred, and greed."

"Kids learn how to fight from watching adults. My parents are especially good teachers."

"Hitting people is easier than listening to them. Working things out is a lot harder than punching somebody out."

"When I'm quiet and nice, nobody pays any attention to me. But if I holler and scream, I get noticed real fast."

"I'd rather argue than admit I'm wrong."

"Sometimes, the reason people fight is they're scared. At least that's why I do."

"I like how it feels when I get even."

"I want my own way, and throwing a fit is the quickest way to get it. It works every time."

"My friends might think I'm a wimp if I didn't stand up for my rights."

Though their explanations are less complex, these are the same basic reasons nations fight. Attempting to justify their warlike actions, one group labels its reasons noble, while those of their adversaries are discredited and dismissed.

Admittedly, it's a perplexing and frustrating question. Why can't everybody just live together in peace? Why do humans fight so much and nations go to war so often?

Perhaps the human race is depraved and rotten to the core. Many would subscribe to this theory and would have us believe that, born in original sin and left to themselves, people can't quit their destructive, violent behavior.

There are also those who preach original blessing; who emphasize that we are born of love, possessing high hopes and filled with amazing potential. If this is so, fighting and wars are not inevitable. Instead, they're the product of the same destructive qualities those school children listed: fear that reveals itself in jealousy, bigotry, and prejudice; the unwillingness to forgive, the failure to be kind and gentle with one another; selfishness that rears its ugly head as greed and possessiveness; deep-seated hostility that produces racism and sexism.

Entire cultures store up and pass on to new generations ancient antagonisms whose original causes are but dimly perceived. Nevertheless, children often retain a refreshing idealism in spite of society's promotion of violence and injustice. Cynical adults (which may include most of us) know these youthful dreams are unrealistic and naive. Utopias have been tried again and again and have always failed. Growing up teaches us firsthand how tough and unyielding the big world can be.

But experience also reveals that the world's a wonderful place, overflowing with beauty and abundance; filled with caring, supportive persons; alive with creative possibilities. How we view reality becomes a matter of focus and perspective.

I choose to think that people could get along together; that wars are not decreed by fate or fixed in the eternal scheme of things. They're options we unwisely choose. Of course there'll always be minor disagreements. But every conflict could, in fact, be resolved, and the human race could live in peace, if everyone practiced radical servanthood as proclaimed and lived by Jesus of Nazareth.

Rather than train our children to be cynical and pessimistic, adults would be well-advised to learn idealism, optimism, wonder, and awe while sitting at their children's feet. A pinch of playfulness would help, too.

## —8—

# WHY DOESN'T GOD GIVE US SOME NEW COMMANDMENTS?

I was a college freshman returning to school by bus after the Thanksgiving holiday. I was anxious and not at all certain I wanted to go back where the food wasn't nearly as appetizing as my mother's, where my roommate snored and had a life-style several light years away from mine, and where I precariously teetered on the brink of flunking calculus.

Bless my parents' hearts. When I wasn't looking, they apparently had slipped a Bible in my backpack. About halfway into my journey, I accidentally found it. Because I was lonely, bored, and had only textbooks to read, I actually spent considerable time studying its pages. No Sunday school teacher pointed at me and said, "It's your turn." We weren't having family devotions where I was pleasantly but firmly instructed to read a passage. This was totally my own decision, an act born of free will.

Until then, Bible study and other spiritual disciplines were chores for me, duties to be endured because of others' expectations. I grudgingly obeyed, but I had never experienced much joy in the process. On that trip I discovered, much to my amazement, that the Bible was filled with wisdom, had messages that spoke just to me, and was rather enjoyable to read.

After all these years, one verse in particular retains its luster in my memory—"For loving God means obeying his commands, and these commands of his are not burdensome" (1 John 5:3, J.B. Phillips). Not burdensome? Not a chore? What a refreshing revelation for a young person! In a flash of divinely given insight, I understood that the commandments of God were not intended to squeeze joy out of my life but to offer it to me abundantly.

The child who asked, "Why hasn't God given us some new commandments?" felt that the old ones were mostly negative and quite difficult to understand. Her argument may have some merit. There are indeed many "Thou shalt nots" and more than a few things have changed since then!

What's needed are not new commandments but fresh interpretations of these ancient rules. The biblical injunctions were never intended to cover every possible condition even in the day they were written, let alone thousands of years later. They would indeed be burdensome if God expected us to follow them slavishly. They were given as guidelines, as principles for living.

The laws of God offer invaluable insights into our daily lives, our actions and relationships. They speak of respect for human life, for persons, and for property. They teach us to live upon the earth reverently and responsibly. They set before us the ways of forgiving love, of justice and righteousness, of gentleness and peace. They plainly state that there are both short-term and eternal consequences for our actions.

God continues to upgrade these principles. The words may remain the same; but by inspiring our human intellect, God suggests new solutions for modern dilemmas. We face agonizingly difficult issues in the fields of medicine, ecology, economics, foreign relations, and a multitude of others, as well as in our personal lives. These call for an outpouring of creative thinking rather than an inflexible adherence to the letter of the law.

Children need to be taught both the historic precepts and the intellectual tools of today. To uncritically dump scriptural commandments on young persons will likely be counterproductive. It makes the rules appear outdated; risks producing guilt; and gives the impression that God's laws are burdens to bear. Without knowledge of these great truths, however, youth will lack a firm foundation on which to build adequate value systems. They need both solid spiritual instruction and the encouragement to use their knowledge in imaginative ways.

The prophet Jeremiah heard God express the essence of the matter: "I will put my law within them, and I will write it on their hearts" (Jeremiah 31:33 NRSV). My life has never been quite the same after that bus trip when God's Word in my mind also became written in my heart.

# —9—

# IF I DIE AS A CHILD, WILL I HAVE TO GO TO SCHOOL IN HEAVEN?

Dear Lindsey,

Thanks for asking such an interesting question about whether or not there's school in heaven. Since I haven't been there yet, I don't know for sure, but I'd like to make a guess. Please be patient with me while I think out loud.

First of all, Lindsey, I certainly hope you don't die young. If you should, however, you'll probably have to go to school. Sorry about that. But school in heaven won't be anything like the one you now attend. There'll be no written assignments, no tests, no report cards, and no tardy slips. Of course, there also won't be any holidays or summer vacation. Here on earth, attendance is required only for young people like you. In heaven everybody will go to school. Even people who die when they're one hundred years old will be in a celestial classroom.

My reason for saying "yes" is that I simply can't imagine heaven being a static, unchanging place where nothing new ever happens. There must be all kinds of exciting things going on with original ideas popping up all over; and the residents must have the most wonderful relationships imaginable. If heaven isn't alive, active, and stimulating, then it just won't be heaven, at least for me. Instead, it would be kind of boring.

Back in biblical times, people talked about heaven by creating word pictures of the most beautiful scenes they could envision. They used images like streets paved with pure gold, walls covered with emeralds and sapphires, and gates made of pearls. A place like that would be rather impressive, but not very cozy or livable. I'd much prefer grass to roll around in, dirt to play with, and maybe a strip of asphalt where I could put a hoop and shoot a few baskets.

There may be some folks who'd enjoy having everything made out of precious metals and rare jewels, but I'd just as soon have a little garden spot where I could grow carrots, tomatoes, and some pumpkins. I've always dreamed of living in a buttercup-dotted meadow, beside a stream with a little waterfall that makes happy gurgling sounds. I'd also like heaven to have a library stocked with the great literary classics, several Agatha Christie mysteries, and a complete collection of Calvin and Hobbes.

What I'm trying to say, Lindsey, is that I think heaven will be a learning experience, the same as your life is right now. But let me tell you, the teachers will really be something. Think about having Sarah and Abraham in person telling about Old Testament events; or sitting at the feet of the prophet Isaiah while he recites magnificent poetry; or listening to David create and sing new psalms. Think about learning American history from Thomas Jefferson and Abraham Lincoln, or science from Madame Marie Curie. How about studying social issues with Dr. Martin Luther King, Jr.? Wouldn't it be a thrill to discuss Native American traditions with Chief Joseph of the Nez Percé tribe? Oh, my, the possibilities are endless!

As far as I'm concerned, that would be heaven. I wouldn't mind going to school one little bit if I could take music theory from Beethoven or Mozart, physics from Albert Einstein, or art from van Gogh. What an inspiration!

I do hope we won't all be expected to play the harp. The harp is okay, but it's not my favorite instrument. I like the violin better, and ever since I was a child, I've thought playing a drum set would be a blast. I suppose if it's necessary, though, I can learn to play and enjoy the harp.

Actually, you won't "have" to go to school in heaven. It will be so special, so very wonderful, you'll *want* to go. You'll be upset if you don't have perfect attendance. Can you imagine the great game at recess where everybody plays and nobody ever gets left out? And we can't forget lunch, now can we? There'll be pepperoni pizza every day, juicy hamburgers, piles of fries with tons of catsup, and chocolate chip cookies still warm from the oven—and no calories whatsoever!

Lindsey, neither one of us is ready to go to heaven, not yet anyway. I'm probably closer than you are, but we've both got too many things to do in this life, and there are lots of people who need us to stick around awhile.

When that moment draws near, I'll get my #2 pencils sharpened and my spiral notebooks ready. I may even sit in the front row, which I never did in regular old earthly school. I usually tried to hide somewhere in the back.

One day, Lindsey, a long, long time from now, you can join me and all the other saints in heaven. We're going to have such fun being in school for eternity! In the meantime, try to enjoy all the learning opportunities you have each day. It'll be good preparation.

Kel

## —10—

# HOW CAN I BE SURE IT'S GOD SPEAKING TO ME?

What are your options when you're heading down the road and aren't quite certain it's the right way? You can keep your eyes peeled for familiar landmarks; make sure you pay attention to all the signs; pull over and chcck a map; ask somebody who hopefully knows the territory; or turn around and go back to where you started. Of course, you can also stubbornly keep going like I've been known to do, mostly because I don't like to admit I might be lost and I'm too proud to ask directions. Sure, it's gotten me into several embarrassing situations. But I'll probably do it again, and no doubt soon.

The stakes in spiritual matters, however, are considerably higher. We're talking about being lost in a way that has eternal consequences. People of all ages ought to ask this question frequently: "How can I be sure it's God speaking to me?" Although it's formulated here as a question, you can easily offer it as a prayer, asking for clarification of God's will, seeking confirmation that you're responding correctly to God's guidance.

Not everyone who claims to hear God's voice and to speak for God is accurately doing so. Most who don't are merely confused. A few, however, may be acting from a self-serving agenda and deliberately trying to lead people astray. A certain amount of skepticism about the spiritual claims of others is healthy. God doesn't mind a bit when we ask tough questions; even when they're bluntly posed, when they're yelled with our fists clenched in anger. If it's an honest question, it will be honored with an honest answer.

Children need to be assured it's quite all right to check out the sources and motives of the directions they receive. Is the message arising from their own desires? Are they yielding to peer pressure? Are they uncritically accepting what adult authority figures tell them?

All of us need to be reminded that God probably doesn't speak in a deep, masculine, booming voice. Lightning bolts and thunder seldom, if ever, accompany God's addresses to humanity. As happened to the prophet Elijah, God's presence is most frequently made known in a still, small voice; in the quiet workings of our consciences; as a hint, a gentle urging, a persistent suggestion. God often acts indirectly to increase our motivation, gives us a vision of the beauty that might be, places a creative idea in our minds, or nudges us to use our active imaginations.

Young persons must be equipped with the conceptual tools for discerning God's will. Sometimes what God wishes for them will be the same as what they want for themselves. At other times, they may have to let go of their own plans before fully embracing God's design.

Historically, one of the most helpful concepts for clarifying God's communication is a four-pronged test devised in the eighteenth century by John Wesley. The first and primary measure is *Scripture*. If God is truly speaking to us, it will be consistent with the overall biblical message.

The second guideline is *tradition*. How have the church, its leaders, scholars, and theologians through the ages understood God's dealings with humanity? Is the way I perceive God leading me in harmony with the basic teachings of the church universal?

Next is *experience*. Have I had outward experiences that confirm my inner feelings? Do I know God loves me, and am I motivated by that love to serve the whole of humanity?

The final standard is *reason*, the critical ability to use our God-given minds. If God is speaking, it may well transcend our human powers of reason, but it will not contradict the highest and best of our intellect.

Used in combination with one another, these four tests—Scripture, tradition, experience, and reason—are valuable when deciding if it's God speaking. When these line up in a semblance of order, a person can be relatively certain that he or she is acting within the will of God.

Kathleen struggled with a difficult decision. While it may have seemed a minor problem to her parents and teachers, it was quite stressful for her. For several months, she'd been feeling led to change her life-style—in particular, how she spent her time. Was she watching too much television and spending more time than necessary on the telephone? Should she devote more time to schoolwork and to helping around the house? If she had the energy to stay up to watch the late night movie, shouldn't she make an extra effort to go to church school the next morning?

She knew the Bible contained frequent references to spending time wisely, to being a good steward of each day. Her friends and family, especially her mom, had suggested she make some changes in what she did with her time. Kathleen herself knew how satisfying it was when she acted more conscientiously and responsibly. And somehow, it all made sense. She was often tired, and twice that week had dozed off in English class. Of course, English was right after lunch, and she sat by a window in the bright sunlight. Still, she knew she was capable of accomplishing a great deal more than she was.

When everything lined up, Kathleen felt sure it was God proposing these adjustments to her daily schedule. Scripture proclaimed it; tradition taught it; her experience was consistent with it; and reason agreed. It was then up to Kathy, with the help of God, to make it happen.

—11—

# WHERE'D ALL THE PROPHETS GO?

Where'd all the prophets go, the great ones of old like Joel, Jeremiah, Isaiah, and John the Baptist? Has God stopped choosing special individuals through which to speak to the church and the world? Perhaps God has gone modern on us and is using videotapes, filmstrips, cassettes, and CDs. I suppose you can reach a lot more people with a multimedia approach. It's considerably more efficient than one person on a soapbox preaching at the top of his or her lungs. Still, the old method has a certain charm.

Those ancient prophets were quite the characters. They knew how to work a crowd and had a flair for the dramatic. To demonstrate how badly God felt when people neglected spiritual matters, they might dress in sackcloth and pour ashes on top of their heads. Okay, so none of them ever made a best-dressed list. They didn't care. Getting people to hear God's word was first and foremost in their minds.

I've always felt sympathy for the three children of the prophet Hosea. To teach the nation a lesson, he gave his offspring symbolic names which in Hebrew meant, "God Sows" (that is, "God Will Punish"), "Not Pitied," and "Not My People." I have difficulty imagining a mother calling her sweet little daughter home by yelling, "Yoo-hoo, Not Pitied, it's time for dinner." It must have been tough for them at school. They either turned out to be wonderful, thoughtful, humble children; or the meanest, toughest kids at the synagogue.

Then there was John the Baptist who lived in the sand dunes, wore a camel-hair outfit, and ate the equivalent of chocolate-covered grasshoppers. When John showed up for the party, people noticed. Of course, folks may have tried to stay upwind of him.

When the prophets spoke, you knew they had a word from God. They didn't mess around with clever little sermonettes sprinkled with crowd-pleasing jokes. Just in case somebody might not get the point, they frequently began their official pronouncements with words to the effect, "Thus saith the Lord." It was certainly a more impressive opening line than, "Hi, folks. How ya' doin'?"

People listened, even though the messages usually came with barbs and made the audience squirm. It was, of course, great entertainment. Movies, video games, and mass market paperbacks hadn't yet been invented. And nobody had thought up Garfield, Bart Simpson, or the Ninja Turtles. An Israelite family might have been sitting at home staring at the dried mud walls when somebody remembered that Amos was prophesying south of town. "Let's go. I hear he's really got his act together. They say he doesn't use notes, either."

Over the millennia, the world has obviously changed. Yet, there may be as many prophets of God today. We simply know them by other names: teacher, pastor, doctor, judge, police officer, counselor, social worker, poet, novelist, political cartoonist, environmentalist, conservationist. Perhaps we forget that those biblical prophets didn't live at the same time. They're all listed in the same book, but they proclaimed God's truth across a thousand years of history. In addition, we have the distinct advantage of hindsight. It's far easier to determine what was and wasn't of God when we look at it from the perspective of centuries later.

Do you suppose there are modern Jonahs pleading with us to be inclusive in our thinking; asking us to lay aside our prejudices and to love our enemies?

Could there be contemporary versions of Hosea calling us to build forgiving, accepting relationships; to make commitments that will stand the test of time?

Have you heard lately of any John the Baptists urging people to adopt a simpler life-style and to return to their spiritual roots?

Are there any twentieth-century Amoses reprimanding the church when its worship is cold and empty; scolding us when we act pompous and proud; challenging us to care for the poor, the homeless, the victims of abuse, the outcasts?

How about an up-to-date model of old Micah, who cried out for a renewal of moral values; who in these days would surely take a strong stand against drug and alcohol abuse; who would eloquently oppose the violence in our society, the cheating, stealing, shoplifting, malicious gossip, and a host of other harmful things we do.

There actually may be more prophetic persons in our midst than in those ancient times. If we no longer notice God's message being spoken, perhaps it's because we aren't listening very well. Opening our eyes, ears, and minds would enable us to receive the prophetic word from such people as Nelson Mandela and Mother Teresa. Institutions and groups have also played prophetic roles in society, from the civil rights movement to women's liberation, to local churches and denominations.

God sometimes speaks to us in novel and surprising ways. It might be a good idea, therefore, to take a peek at Dr. Seuss's books and to get acquainted with Pogo, Charlie Brown, the Muppets, and some of their friends.

## —12—

# DO I HAVE TO GO TO CHURCH?

Over the years, I've probably heard them all. One or two excuses may have escaped my attention. But I'm really quite knowledgeable, since I tried most of them myself when I was a kid.

"How come I have to go to church? None of my friends' parents make them go."

"I don't like my Sunday school teacher. He expects me to answer his dumb questions and take part in class discussions."

"I have a hard time sitting still for the whole church service. The sermon is usually boring and the prayers are way too long. I'll bet not even God listens all the way to the amen."

"Do I have to go? No offense, Dad, but the music is for tired old geezers who like their songs in slow motion."

"Come on, Mom, give me a break. I'm just a growing kid who needs more sleep. What's that you say? Don't stay up so late and go to bed earlier? I couldn't do that. I'd miss 'Saturday Night Live.'"

"Maybe I'd go if they served soft drinks at the social hour. I don't feel wanted when all they have are coffee and tea."

There's frequently a pinch of truth in their reasoning as well as a great deal of creative thought. They'd get straight "A's" if they worked as hard on their schoolwork. Parents, therefore, need to work a bit harder and come up with even more imaginative answers. The ultimate goal, of course, is to produce self-motivated young persons who want to participate in the church.

When children are young and innocent, they are often eager to attend. They may enthusiastically drag the rest of the family along on those Sundays when everyone else would rather sleep in. If by some miracle you have a child who, even at age thirteen, never asks if she or he has to go to church, count your many blessings.

As soon as their young minds encounter the big, wide world, they usually start thinking independently. This is both a blessing and a source of considerable parental stress. They're able to make more and more of their own decisions. But they also learn how to argue intelligently and disagree convincingly.

At certain stages of development, many of them become embarrassed by being seen in public with their parents. Worship is about as public as you can get, sitting there in front of God and everybody while the old folks sing off-key, pray out loud, and keep giving them a "this is good for you" look.

I'm well qualified to tell you the correct ways to respond to this dilemma. Our children are grown and nearly out of the nest. (The definition of an expert is one whose lion-taming theories are formulated while looking at animal picture books rather than living in a lions' den.) Though I make light of the problem, it is serious and has probably produced a fair amount of high blood pressure, along with raised, whining voices on any given Sunday morning.

From the "For What It's Worth Department," here are my "Do-I-have-to-go-to-church?" guidelines.

1. Clarify what they're really asking. The refusal to attend church one Sunday, or even a year of Sundays, should not be equated with atheism. What sounds to parents like excuses may be seen by children as legitimate reasons. Keep an open mind. Take time to listen and to talk it through.

2. Don't assume you'll be dealing with this question only once or twice. Seventy times seven is more like it. Even if you formulate the most profound response in the history of the world, rivaling the Gettysburg Address in literary value, they'll still ask the question again, probably at 8:00 A.M. that very next Sabbath. Kids are patient people. They can wait forever in hopes of discovering a tiny chink in your parental armor. It is irrelevant that you've told your child, "Yes, you're going to church," for 227 Sundays in a row, through rain, hail, snow, and sleet. On number 228, they'll pop the question once more, most likely when your mouth is filled with hot coffee and toast so you'll have something

on which to choke. Be prepared. One of the essential requirements of parenting is to be more patient than they are.

Strive to accept the truth that they're supposed to ask this question. It's inspired and ordained by God who constantly urges youth toward independence. It's God's way of ensuring that their's will not be a hand-me-down faith, but a deeply personal, vital experience. God, of course, feels compassion for harried parents, but that's not enough to stop this process of growth that's as old as life itself. Yes, it's aggravating, but it's part of the divine plan.

3. Avoid the following unproductive responses:

—The Hurt Parent Routine. "It's okay if you don't go (sniff, sniff). I'll just sit alone on that hard, cold pew. I don't mind."

—The John Wayne School of Child Rearing. "Now listen, and listen good, pilgrim. You're going to church or else it's you and me, kid, at high noon by the corral. Do I make myself clear?"

—The Fire and Brimstone Lecture Series. "God won't like it if you don't go. Stay home if you must, but if you see lightning, you'd better duck."

—The Sleezy Salesperson Technique. "Have I got a deal for you. If you accept my offer of going to church, I'll cook your food and wash your clothes until you're eighteen or on your own, whichever comes later. But wait, there's more. You can eat your dessert even when you don't finish your vegetables. How's that sound? Have we got a deal?"

4. My final piece of advice is to trust God. You aren't the only ones in the universe who love that child. God does and will provide other persons to help nurture and guide him or her. You need to do your level best. But recognize that, like all parents, you will make your share of mistakes. One day you'll be a little too lenient, the next a bit too strict. You're human. That's why God appoints a host of people to help you raise these youthful bundles of potential: aunts, uncles, older siblings, grandparents, teachers, pastors, storytellers, coaches, scouting leaders, and on and on.

When a child nails you with a question like, "Why do I have to go to church?" the best answer is a quiet, honest response. "Because I love you and want the best for you. Because God would like a special time with you in a place where you can feel close to God."

While you madly rush around trying to find their clean socks, that lost tennis shoe, iron the blouse that was thrown on the floor in a heap, and braid hopelessly tangled hair, take a deep breath and practice OTJ (on the job) prayer. It'll be worth the effort even if it means looking thrown together yourself. God will understand.

# —13—

## IS GOD INVISIBLE OR IS IT JUST A TRICK?

Once upon a time a cute little tumbleweed, round as round could be, lived in a field with wild daisies, buttercups, and dandelions. Each of them produced beautiful blossoms while she did nothing but sit there on her stalk growing ever more plump. It was hard for her to be patient. She became increasingly anxious to fulfill her purpose in life. If she couldn't bloom, she at least wanted to travel and see the world. Even a short trip as far as the bend in the road would be better than this.

She worried that she must be doing something wrong. Maybe she wasn't working hard enough at being a good tumbleweed. Suppose there'd been tumbling lessons when she was a seedling and she'd missed them? "What's the point of being a tumbleweed if all I ever do is stay in one place like a big lump?"

The days grew shorter and the nights cooler. As the leaves on nearby trees turned gold, orange, and crimson, she felt a stirring in her branches. She began swaying to and fro. Glancing about, she couldn't see what was causing her vibrations. Unknown to her, she was about to be set free. Suddenly, her stem twisted and snapped. She did a graceful somersault, then tried a cartwheel. It was such fun! Soon she was merrily bouncing down the street, off on the journey of her long cherished dreams.

"Whee-e-e," she exclaimed as she raced across a meadow. "I don't know what's happening to me, but I love it!" She decided to rest against a wooden fence for a few moments to catch her breath. Soon, other tumbleweeds joined her. "Can you tell me whom to thank for my marvelous adventure?" she asked.

"Why, the brisk autumn wind, of course," they replied.

"But I don't see anything. How can something invisible give me a new life and make me feel so joyful?"

"It's a wonderful mystery. You can't see the wind; and no matter how hard you try, you can't grab a handful of it. Seek to put it in a jar, and it will be gone before the lid's in place. Even though it's not visible, it's still very real."

"Oh, I know that. I can feel its presence. Well, I've got to be going. I have so much to do and so many places to go. Good-bye for now, my friends." With that, she peeked around the edge of the fence and was off and tumbling once again.

We humans can't see God any more than a tumbleweed can see the wind. Yet we can clearly observe what God does. The universe is absolutely crammed with signs of God's activity. We are surrounded by beauty, filled with love, and given gifts in abundance. The invisible God is revealed in every blade of grass, in every droplet of water, in every cloud and mountain, every star and planet. Most of all, God's presence is made known in people; in their kind words, twinkling eyes, smiles, hugs, and kisses. Where persons love and care and serve, there is God.

Nearly two thousand years ago, a very perceptive person named the apostle Paul taught that visible things are temporary and not really very important. Invisible things, he said, like faith and peace, last forever and are valuable beyond reckoning. The things we can see are physical in nature and can be in only one place at any given moment. If God's being were actually visible to our human eyes, God would be limited by time and space just as we are.

It's no trick. God is invisible. It's how it has to be in order for God to be with everyone everywhere. It also makes it possible for each of us to "see" God in exactly the way we need. People who feel guilty from doing wrong experience God as a forgiving parent. Those who are scared and lonely know God as the Good Shepherd, a source of comfort. Those who are confused feel God as their guide and counselor. Those who are happy discover that God rejoices and laughs with them. Because God is an invisible presence, God is able to love each of us as a unique, one of a kind individual.

It was a stroke of genius on God's part, wasn't it?

# —14—

## WHO MADE GOD?

When I was four, I'm told I tagged along after my mother, tugging on her dress, repeatedly asking, "Who made God? Where did God come from? What was there before there was God? When did God start?" Somehow, she remained a calm, peaceful person and never once threatened to tape my mouth shut, although she may have seriously considered it. No doubt she was much relieved each day when my bedtime arrived and her little bundle of questions was finally quieted. Though I was apparently something of a pest, I can take solace in the knowledge that at least I asked interesting questions.

My mother might have had the urge to set me down and say, "Listen, young man, why can't you be like other children and ask normal questions like, 'May I go out and play? Do I have to eat my peas and carrots? Why can't I have a pet boa constrictor?' "

However, "Who made God?" is a common and frequently asked question by young people the world over. It obviously has variations and different flavors; but its essence remains constant. "Who is this God-person I hear so much about? I can tell whoever it is must really be important. But nobody will ever tell me where God came from. Why not?"

The answer is: there is no answer. Many questions our human minds are capable of asking do not have satisfying answers. The universe in which we live is filled with mysteries and enigmas. Through persistent study and research, some of them will eventually be solved. Yet no matter how hard we try, mysteries will surely remain that may never yield their secrets to even the cleverest of minds.

The best response to bright, inquisitive children is an honest, "I don't know." But don't let that be the end of the dialogue. Talk about how it feels *not* to know something—how it can be very frustrating, a source of wonder and awe, or a mixture of both.

Some twenty-five hundred years ago, Moses had a personal encounter with this particular dilemma. He'd fled from Egypt after getting in a bit of trouble. God appeared to him in a burning bush and asked him to go back to lead the Hebrew people to freedom. "Okay," said Moses, "but tell me your name, otherwise no one will believe or follow me."

"I AM WHO I AM," replied God.

"What kind of name is that?" complained Moses.

"The best I can do on short notice."

"Oh, wonderful. I'm going to convince people to leave their familiar surroundings in Egypt and wander for forty years through the wilderness by telling them 'I AM' sent me? Right."

"Moses, I'm not a thing with a noun for a name. I'm a Being, a personal God, so use verbs to describe me. I am love; I am peace; I am life."

"That's just great," murmured Moses. "I was never very good with verbs. Couldn't you make up a fancy name with a bunch of initials after it, like B.S., M.A., LL.D., and Ph.D.? Something to impress the folks?"

"Nope."

"I didn't think so."

"Get a move on, Moses! There's work to be done."

Like Moses, we want a theology that's nice and tidy, that clearly explains all the mysteries of the universe. We'd like scientific precision in every realm of life, including the spiritual, emotional, and artistic. It is not to be. The deepest, most profound realities will forever be wrapped, at least partially, in mystery.

We are called to respond by faith, accepting the truth of God with our whole lives, and not with our rational selves alone. We don't need to know who made God to experience God's marvelous grace in our lives. We are not required to compose a systematic theology in order to feel God's love. There are times and circumstances when the appropriate action is to kneel in humility rather than to analyze; to worship and celebrate rather than attempt to explain. In moments of wonder, it is enough to take off one's shoes, stand still, and get goose bumps from head to toe.

Don't be afraid of children's tough questions to which even the wisest philosophers and theologians have no answers. Use your imagination. Make wild guesses. Quote poetry. Paint word pictures. Do what I call "dreamthinking." Then have a few good laughs at your own expense and offer a basic affirmation of faith.

"For God so loved the world. . . ."

"Jesus loves me, this I know. . . ."

"[Nothing] in all creation, will be able to separate us from the love of God in Christ Jesus our Lord" (Romans 8:39 NRSV).

Finally, give that child a big bear hug. It may provide you with a bonus: a few minutes' rest before the next round of perplexing, impossible questions begin!

# —15—

## IS GOD A BOY OR A GIRL?

When I was a lad of six or seven years, I spent the better part of a summer dressing up in women's clothing. It was such fun! We had inherited an attic full of turn-of-the-century fashions, vintage 1900 apparel, replete with ostrich plume and peacock feather hats, silk gowns, elbow-length gloves, and a marvelous assortment of high heels. I spent magical hours parading in front of my sister's long mirror, admiring my beauty. The satin shoes didn't fit my child-sized feet, causing me to make loud clop-clop noises as I shuffled across the hardwood floor. My parents may have silently wondered about their son's sexual identity.

Along with modeling petticoats, however, I wrestled with my father, played a rough-and-tumble brand of football, built pretend roads, and dreamed of being a truck driver. I eventually grew to be a rather masculine person, if I do say so myself.

Yet I freely acknowledge my feminine side. I highly value the caring, nurturing, sensitive part of my personality. I feel warm and tender when holding a baby. I take pride in being a good cook, in knowing how to clean a house efficiently, in being able to sort dark from light clothes, in comforting a child by kissing an "ouchie."

Having a feminine dimension makes me no less masculine. In fact, it enables me to be a complete human. I find that acknowledging my wholeness is very rewarding and fulfilling.

No less an authority than the Bible tells us that we are created in the divine image. Our powers of deduction indicate, therefore, that God, who makes us male and female, must be both masculine and feminine. It further follows that we are most God-like when expressing these two qualities in an appropriate and balanced manner.

The biblical record offers a wealth of imagery. On the masculine side, we read of God as King; the Mighty One of Israel, a warrior; he who breaks the bow and shatters the spear; the great authority figure who utters commandments; the all-knowing judge; the One we call our forgiving Father.

The feminine representations tell of the God who enfolds us to her bosom; who lovingly prepares meals; who gathers us under her wings as a hen does her chicks; who binds up the brokenhearted, seeks the lost, and patiently waits for those who have wandered.

In Western categories of thinking, we crave either/or answers. We assume that if God is masculine, God cannot be feminine. And if God is feminine in nature, that would preclude expressions of masculinity. But what if God is both Our Father and Our Mother—the One who rules with righteousness and justice, yet who holds our hand in the valley of the shadow? Perhaps God is both a strict disciplinarian and the tender One who showers us with hugs and kisses.

In this, as in many questions our children ask, we must deal with the limitations of language. English, in particular, has only gender restricted or plural pronouns. It has led to an exclusive use of masculine references for God, causing women to feel left out and men to feel vaguely guilty and incomplete. Until clever semanticists create new pronouns, we must do our best with the words we have. It does not hinder us, however, from viewing God as the Great Both/And, as our Father and our Mother.

The question, "Is God a boy or a girl?" needs to be rephrased to read, "In what ways is God both a boy and a girl?" Our saving grace may be a sense of humor, as in the case of an inquisitive child who asked a parent this very question.

"Well, dear, I'm not sure. Maybe God is both a boy and a girl."

"Oh, I get it. God can go to the bathroom standing up or sitting down."

## —16—

# WHERE'S THE CROSS-EYED BEAR?

Listening is a rare and vanishing art. Perhaps it has always been in short supply. Unhappily, there simply aren't enough quality listeners to go around. The number of people who want and need to talk far exceeds those who are skilled at listening. While a helpful exercise, talking to oneself isn't as satisfying as having real persons that come complete with facial expressions.

All sorts of people hear God's call to speak, to preach, and to proclaim; but few persons seem to hear God's call to witness by being good listeners. Maybe it's because listening is such a difficult discipline. Hearing is what you do with your ears. Listening involves actively employing your whole heart and mind and soul. It's hard work when done properly. No offense to the apostle Paul, but shouldn't listening have been included as one of the fruits of the Spirit in Galatians 5:22?

Listening is an absolutely necessary ingredient in the communication process. Without it, messages become hopelessly garbled; speakers' intentions are easily misinterpreted; nuances in conversations are totally missed. As an illustration, children in worship may not always understand what's being said and sung. They need kindly, sympathetic ears to help them make sense of the many verbal complexities and confusions.

During my growing-up years, Sunday afternoon dinner was an important family affair and a workshop in communication. Father was a preacher in rural communities and frequently did double duty as the custodian. It meant being the last ones to leave the church building. As soon as we got home, we all pitched in to prepare the noon meal as quickly as possible. For some reason, going to church works up a ravenous appetite in people. After our initial hunger pangs were satisfied, our discussions began, often by telling Father the various mistakes he'd made. He managed to be gracious about what, in retrospect, I know must have been a humbling ordeal.

When my sister and I were grade school youngsters, we shared our naive, honest, and often amusing impressions of worship. One Sunday Anna asked, "Where's the cross-eyed bear Daddy talked about? I looked everywhere but never saw it."

With quizzical looks, both our mother and father responded in unison. "The what?"

"The cross-eyed bear. You talked about it a bunch of times, Daddy."

"I did? When?"

"In your sermon, that's when. I heard you with my own two ears. Don't you believe me?" She was starting to get a bit irritated.

"Yes, dear, I believe you, but maybe you heard something differently than I said it. Or perhaps I didn't speak clearly enough." Then he whispered to himself, "What do you suppose I said?"

"Well," answered Mother, "you preached about the need to bear our crosses."

"I'll bet that's it! I mentioned the cross Jesus bore and the cross I bear. The cross-eyed bear, get it?"

Meanwhile, I had spit out a mouthful of green beans from laughing so hard. I probably shouldn't have acted so uncharitably toward my sister. After all, I had made more than my share of youthful goofs and blunders; and, as later events would document, I committed a multitude more.

For example, there was that Easter when the ham and mashed potatoes were being passed. I asked what Jesus thought he was doing in the gravy in the first place. I had a pretty good idea what would happen to me if I played around in a bowl of gravy. It would be a messy and unsanitary thing to do. I figured Jesus' parents should have taught him better.

"I'll bet they didn't even have gravy back then," interjected my sister.

"Sure they did. We sang about it this morning."

"Son, I think you must be talking about the chorus to 'Christ Arose.'" I thought I detected a chuckle or two. "What it actually says is, 'Up from the grave he arose.'" It was my sister's turn to spit out food, except she was too polite for such gross behavior and used her napkin.

We usually talked about who was and who wasn't in church that morning. The "wasn'ts" often got more mention. Were there valid reasons they weren't in their regular spots? Was somebody in the family sick? Were they mad at anybody, anybody usually meaning Father? How many Sundays in a row had they missed? I was the one who wanted to know how much the absentees usually put in the offering plate, and would we get paid if they ended up going to the church down the block?

There are lessons to be learned from conversations such as these with our children: the importance of enunciating clearly; the need to make certain your hearers have accurately heard your words and grasped your motives. Kids, of course, aren't the only ones who mix up messages. All of us need to hone our listening skills, practice seeing the comical side of the things we say, and maintain our spiritual health with massive daily doses of humility.

To this day I have trouble singing, "O for a Thousand Tongues to Sing," with a straight face. More than four decades ago I envisioned a giant mouth from outer space with a thousand wagging tongues inside. It would have been a sight to behold!

Then there was that Monday when my sister and I came home from school for the lunch hour. Though she was normally a very deliberate eater, she devoured her meal quickly. "If you're done, Anna, you may be excused."

"I'm not going anywhere until I get some pie," she immediately responded.

"But we don't have any pie, dear. I didn't bake yesterday. How about some cookies instead?"

"I don't want any cookies. I want pie. In church yesterday you promised we'd have pies today."

"I don't remember saying anything about pies. When did you think I did?"

"During the last hymn. You kept singing 'some pies tomorrow, some pies tomorrow.' I'd like either apple or chocolate cream."

Mother looked at Father in exasperation, as if to say, "Do something, she's your daughter." They leaned toward each other for a brief parental conference.

"Anna, I'm sorry. The song you thought was 'Some Pies Tomorrow' was actually 'Sunrise, Tomorrow.'"

"That's okay, but I'd still like a piece of pie. Cherry will do."

## —17—

## WHO SAYS SO?

A high-powered lawyer tried to put Jesus on the spot, hoping to make him look bad in front of his friends and students. "What do I have to do," he asked, "to get into heaven?" Jesus answered by asking two questions of his own.

"You've read what the scriptures say about it, haven't you? Well, what's your opinion?"

"I don't know. That's why I'm asking you. I'm familiar with those rules about loving God with all your heart and your neighbor as yourself. But I get confused. Who exactly is my neighbor?"

In order to make the answer clear and unforgettable, Jesus told the lawyer a story. It's called the parable of the good Samaritan. When he got to the punch line, which in its element of surprise surpassed anything O. Henry ever thought up, Jesus asked yet another question.

"Which of these three people, the priest, Levite, or Samaritan, proved to be a neighbor to the robbery victim?" The attorney responded with the obvious answer, the Samaritan. "Gotcha," said Jesus. "Now it's your turn to go into the world and act the same."

Jesus was skilled at gently but firmly dealing with folks who kept saying, "Who says so?" Like the lawyer, they used a variety of questions and were usually subtle about it. But their actual motives were transparent to Jesus. What they really wanted to ask was, "Where do you come off speaking for God?" And "Who do you think you are to criticize our religious practices and lifestyle?"

One of Jesus' frequent and favorite methods of answering a question was to ask a question. "Who says so?" was likely to get a "Why do you want to know?" in return. It placed responsibility where it belonged—with the person doing the asking. Jesus never avoided giving sincere answers to honest queries. Sometimes, though, he wanted to give inquirers the opportunity to answer their own questions. He knew they had the answers. They simply needed a perceptive person to draw out the truth already within them.

The authority of Jesus was inner and spiritual. He didn't recite long lists of rules and regulations, brag about going to a prestigious rabbinical school, or pull rank in any other way. He spoke from the heart. When somebody cornered him and asked, "Who says so?", Jesus never replied with a defensive, "I do, that's who!"

In daily family life, children frequently ask, "Who says so?" As annoying as this may be for busy, tired parents, it should be handled as graciously as possible. Avoid autocratic responses that cut off discussion, cause frustration, and build resentment. Save "Because I say so!" for dire emergencies only.

Borrow a page from the way of Jesus. Ask a question right back. It's a particularly effective and disarming approach, especially for potentially divisive topics. Before leaping to your own defense, find out what the other person feels, thinks, and believes.

"Who says so?" is basically a struggle to determine who's in charge. It's a fair question for people of all ages to ask. God has never seemed to be bothered by it, even when Old Testament prophets raised their clenched fists toward the heavens and demanded to know "How come?" As the ultimate authority in our lives, God is never authoritarian, arbitrary, or capricious. The Divine Being is wonderfully gentle and consistent.

Openness is a worthy goal for adults who live and work with children. A dogmatic approach may gain short-term results; but over the long haul, responses that engage other persons in decision making are far more productive. The desired objective is not the uncritical obedience of the small person to the big person. Rather it is helping individuals young and old alike attain their highest potential and achieve their maximum inner growth. The climate most conducive for this is one of mutual respect, honesty, freedom of expression, and trust.

We must all learn to accept external controls, checks, and balances. They're a reality at nearly every turn. However, if outward rules are our primary motivation, we will sooner or later become cranky, grouchy people. What we truly want for our children, our youth, and ourselves is the wisdom to turn all the "ought-to's" into "want-to's." Those who do are on their way to a life filled with deep relationships, rich experiences, and abiding joy.

# —18—

# WHY DON'T PEOPLE STOP POLLUTING THE EARTH?

While unloading the back of our station wagon, I overheard a fascinating and wise conversation among materials waiting to be recycled.

"This is my first time at the center," said a cardboard box nervously.

"Don't worry," an aluminum can assured her. "I've been here more than ten times."

"That's impressive, but I'm still scared. Listen to those terrible noises."

"I know. I was frightened at first, too. Relax, you'll be fine. They have to crunch, break, and melt us down before we can be made into wonderful new containers. It's exciting for me to wonder what kind of soda pop can I'll be next. Before you know it, you'll be a fresh box with no scrapes, dents, or smudges."

A fragmented old newspaper resting nearby joined the discussion. "I'm just happy to be here. I was in a ditch alongside a busy highway for over three years. Finally, a youth group came by and cleaned everything up, including me."

"It's no fun being trashed, I can tell you. Why do people force us into a life of garbage?" A cute glass jar was talking. "It doesn't take any more effort to recycle us than to throw us away."

"You're right. They can make extra money, too. A bag filled with me and my buddies," offered the aluminum can, "is worth several dollars."

"Then why don't more humans recycle us?" asked a magazine with yellowed edges. "Are they really that lazy?"

"You better believe it!" exclaimed the whole group.

"I don't think they want to be bothered," a plastic foam plate suggested.

"Plus they must really be dumb," the jar chimed in. "Don't they know the ozone layer has so many holes it looks like Swiss cheese? Can't they see how toxic their dumps are, how smelly their smog is, and how slimy their water's become? The earth's soon going to be in a terrible pickle, and they simply don't understand what a serious situation it is."

"And most of them seem to prefer it that way," added a discarded catalogue. "Ignorance, they claim, is bliss. Ha!"

"It's mostly a problem of vision," the jar said. "They want what's convenient for them. Humans are notoriously shortsighted and apparently don't care what happens to the future."

"Future my pop-top!" interjected the can. "We're talking about a major crisis right now. A lot of the trouble has to do with making a profit. Companies think it's cheaper for consumers to throw us away. They don't sell as much when people repair things. And I suppose it takes a little longer to recycle. Humans are fond of saying, 'Time is money.'"

"Haven't they heard, 'You can pay me now or pay me later?'" asked a used telephone book.

The cardboard box who had been quietly listening, spoke up. "Probably. Obviously, when it comes to the environment, they don't believe it. Humans can be a rather arrogant species. They think because God put them in charge of the world, they can do anything they jolly well please. They act as if there's an endless supply of natural resources. Boy, are they in for a rude awakening! Maybe people are afraid to change, sort of like how I was feeling. It isn't easy to let go of what's familiar and comfortable to you."

"I know, but they better start learning," advised the newspaper. "Time is running out. I'm quite well-read on the subject, you know. I also wonder if too many people have negative attitudes. They don't think their actions matter. I've heard them say, 'I'm just one person, what can I do?'"

"Hey, they caused the problem," interjected the can. "This mess sure didn't happen by itself. Each and every one of them must bear part of the responsibility. There's more than enough power to solve everything if they'd all pitch in."

The cardboard box shyly scooted forward. "I didn't realize how important all of this is. I'm still a little scared, but I'm ready now to be recycled. See you guys in our next life."

# —19—

## DID GOD NOTICE THAT MY FOLKS DIDN'T PUT ANYTHING IN THE OFFERING PLATE?

Church Headquarters
Division of Solutions and Answers

Dear Official Problem Solver and Answer Giver:

I need your advice really bad. I don't know where else to turn. It happened last Sunday during the church service. I was so embarrassed. Everyone in our row put money in the collection plate; everyone, that is, except my parents. I probably shouldn't have looked, but I did and there were lots of twenties, quite a few checks, and even a hundred dollar bill. My folks passed the plate on real quick. I'll bet God and at least half of the congregation noticed. The usher kind of raised an eyebrow as if to say, "Are you guys deadbeats, or what?" I almost expected him to hand the plate back until we put something in. The whole experience made me want to crawl under the pew and not come out until worship was over and everybody had gone home. I toughed it out, but wouldn't you know the sermon was on stewardship and the importance of tithing?

What do I do now? How can I ever go back to church and face my friends? Would it be okay to sit in the back row of the balcony and sneak out before the benediction? Most of all, I want to quit feeling so guilty. I don't blame God for being mad at us; but

I need to know if God holds grudges; and if the answer is yes, for how long?

Signed,
Anxious Youth

P.S. How come your Division of Solutions and Answers has only one worn-out answering machine, a battered manual typewriter, and you as its part-time staff person; while the Department of Church Conflict, Woe, and Grief has a hundred phone lines, fifty post office boxes, twenty-five fax machines, and two hundred secretaries?

Dear Anxious:

Regarding your problem, let me respond on several levels. First, God does not hold grudges; never has, never will. God probably noticed that your folks didn't put anything in the plate, but God certainly won't hound you. As a matter of fact, God doesn't want you to feel guilty about it at all. God wouldn't use guilt to make you do something even as a last resort. People may nag you sometimes, but not God.

God wants you to feel good about yourself. What others in the congregation think is their own problem, not yours. You just hold your head high, and next time, tell that usher to put his eyebrow back where it belongs. God always motivates us in positive, affirming ways—like sending a beautiful rainbow or sunrise, having somebody give us a great big hug, or sending a friend to offer a word of encouragement.

Forget all that stuff you've been told about how God will "get you" if you don't do what you're supposed to do. Sure, God expects everybody to be their very best, to love and serve and do their fair share. But relax; there isn't some huge ledger or grade book in heaven where your deeds are recorded for posterity. As far as God is concerned, each day is a brand new beginning.

Wouldn't it be wonderful if we humans acted the same way God does—no guilt trips, no trying to get even, no scare tactics? It might help you feel better to remember how Jesus lived and what he taught. Never once in the Gospels is Jesus quoted as saying, "Give me your money first, then I'll help you." Jesus offered God's grace freely, generously, and without conditions. If you needed help, Jesus simply reached out to help. Simple as that. It didn't matter to him how much or how little you put in the offering plate.

Faith is an inside job. God doesn't beat you over the head to force you to obey. God gently warms your heart until you want to do what's right. Let me share a Bible verse from Romans 8:1. You'll like it. "There is therefore now no condemnation for those who are in Christ Jesus" (NRSV). Believe it!

To answer your postscript, I'm going to ask you a question: how come there's ten times more bad news in the media than good news? Could it be that people enjoy griping, complaining, and being negative more than they do helping, caring, and being positive? Think about it, and write again soon.

Peace,

Part-time Staff Person
Division of Solutions and Answers

## —20—

# I PRAYED FOR A PUPPY AND NEVER GOT ONE. WHAT GIVES?

Dear God, Please send me a puppy. I'd like one with fluffy hair and floppy ears, who'll play with me and sleep in my bed. Amen."

His mother had heard variations of this theme every evening for the past three weeks. She and his father had tried to tell him that it couldn't be. There'd be no dog until they moved out of the apartment complex where pets weren't allowed, and that would likely be a year or more. For their son it might as well be an eternity. Anyway, he wasn't in a mood to listen to their words of caution, which, understandably, were as gentle as could be. His mom and dad spent several late nights wondering how to tell their innocent, trusting child that God wasn't going to grant his wish.

Children's prayers are often refreshing in their candor and amusing by their creative, colorful expressions. The prayer of one sincere child may be more pleasing to God than all the collects and formal confessions in the history of the church laid end to end. God is not much impressed by proper sentence structure, literary merit, large vocabulary, or eloquent delivery. A pure heart, honest motives, and a receptive spirit are what matter to God.

It's quite possible for people of all ages to pray with childlike trust and openness. Children aren't the only ones capable of using simple, direct language. Prayer at its highest is conversational and natural, very much like talking with a dear friend about the day's events, about problems and pains, hopes and dreams.

The prayers that truly bless me make me feel almost as though I've invaded the speaker's privacy. They have a level of intimacy reserved for those who are deeply in love, who even get mushy now and again.

Regardless of how experienced and skilled a person may be in communicating with God, the dilemma of unanswered prayer is certain to surface sooner or later. For example, I have been praying for peace on earth for most of my adult life. Yet every time I turn around, some nation or ethnic group has taken up arms against another. Hasn't God been listening to my requests? Haven't I been praying hard enough? It makes me wonder sometimes what I've been doing wrong. The Bible says that if I pray believing, my requests will be granted. Well, I've been believing in peace for what seems to me a long while, and praying as earnestly as I know how.

Of course, the Scriptures don't specify when our requests will be granted. Part of the solution to unanswered prayer may be our own impatience. We want instant results. We prayed for it yesterday; we expect an answer by tomorrow; and in the affirmative, of course. God, however, is patient, long-suffering, and acts according to a divine timetable.

God is moved by our heartfelt prayers but always keeps open the options of replying with a "yes," "no," or "not yet." Frequently, God seems to ask us to wait until the right time. It's a hard lesson for wide-eyed, hopeful children to learn. Waiting is difficult for the most mature among us, and particularly so for many youngsters.

"I've been praying for a puppy," that child no doubt complained, "and still don't have one. What gives?" With all the facts at hand, we know there are good reasons why his wish cannot be granted. Perhaps his parents also feel their son isn't quite ready for the responsibility of helping to care for one of God's small creatures.

Here was a lad who faithfully knelt beside his bed every night for weeks, pouring out his young soul in the presence of the Almighty. It's very important that his faith in God be nurtured and sustained in the face of disappointment. He and all God's people need to be reminded that prayer is not a form of coercion or a technique of demanding that God do what we want.

Although Jesus did promise "Ask and it will be given you," he was not advertising a celestial vending machine.

Prayer is opening oneself to the will of God. It is listening as much as talking, maybe even more so. Prayer is being in tune with God's purposes. It is the soul's resonance when life is in complete harmony with the divine plan.

Prayer is seeing things through the "eyes of God." By praying we're enabled to understand the big picture of what's best for the whole of creation. God, who is love, must balance one person's desires with the needs of humanity and with concern for the environment. God may not be able to give us exactly what we want in order to give us what we truly need.

I hope some day soon there'll be a puppy in that boy's life. In the meantime, he should be encouraged to continue praying to God in the same eager and expectant way. We all need reminders to make our prayers frequent, fresh, and lively.

## —21—

## I HAD TROUBLE LOVING MY SISTER. HOW CAN GOD EXPECT ME TO LOVE MY ENEMY?

I loved my sister. I really did. For that matter, I still do. But in our younger years, I had interesting ways of letting her know. She had the misfortune of being born four years before I made my grand entry into the world. This was a perfect age differential to make me a pesky, bothersome, ornery little brother. Believe me, I used it to maximum advantage. Just ask her. Decades later, I'm sure she still has vivid memories, if not occasional nightmares, of my shenanigans.

I've always felt that my being a pest was partly justified, sort of payback for her being so perfect. She was the quintessential obedient child: played Mozart sonatas from memory when she was five; never earned a grade lower than A minus in school; always cleaned her plate and didn't try to sneak bread crusts and icky vegetables to the dog; had clean fingernails; never lost a frog or snake in the house; and had no popcorn kernels, rotten apple cores, or cookie crumbs under her covers.

Oh, I sometimes behaved lovingly toward her, but mostly when I wanted a favor like her share of dessert. About the only vice she had was failing to make her bed every morning. She maybe missed doing so once a month. As I saw it, she deserved me. It was a real pain trying to follow in her footsteps. She set an impossibly high standard. People expected me to be equally talented and good. It simply wasn't possible. Therefore, I had no choice but to do naughty things to assert my individuality and to let folks know I was the normal kid in our family.

My mission in life was to keep her humble. I did an admirable job. Without me around, she probably would have become insufferably arrogant. I also take credit for causing a second vice to creep into her personality: a burning desire for vengeance.

One Sunday after I'd been unusually terrible, I went to church school, and what did I hear? The teacher read from Matthew something-or-other about how Jesus said we have to love our enemies. "Maybe the printers made a mistake in the Bible," I suggested. "It could happen, you know."

"Maybe, but not in this case," the teacher replied. "Jesus said it and you better believe it."

"I'll bet he had his fingers crossed."

"Wrong again. Jesus meant every word he ever spoke."

"Well, he wouldn't have said it if he'd had a sister like mine. That's for sure."

"Sh-h-h-h, that's enough. Why don't you read the next paragraph in this morning's lesson?"

"I would if I knew which page we were on." I thought I heard the teacher let out a sigh. I wondered then as I wonder now, how God can expect us to love our enemies when we do so poorly loving our own sisters and brothers. But God does! Nobody ever said loving others would be easy. In fact, the Bible consistently reminds us of the sacrifices involved. Anything as important as love necessarily requires commitment and dedication. God calls us to love unconditionally and with a concern that embraces all of humanity.

It might help if we were to banish the word *enemy* from our language and remove it from all our dictionaries. As soon as we begin to love someone, he or she ceases to be an enemy and becomes a friend, an ally, a companion on the journey. That person may not realize it for awhile; but sooner or later, love will break down the walls, bridge the gaps, and surmount all the barriers. If I refuse to label people as strangers, foes, adversaries, or enemies, I thereby rob those words of their power to hurt and to separate.

All human beings go through awkward stages during which they're not particularly lovable. But that's okay. We aren't loved because we're wonderful and deserving. We're loved because we're needy and can't survive without it. Some of us, I suppose, are less appealing than others. Teenagers, for example, have parts of them growing so rapidly that other parts can't keep pace. It produces a lack of both physical and emotional coordination.

What kind of love would it be, though, if I love only those who love me, who agree with my views, who like how I dress, appreciate the music I listen to, and laugh at all my jokes?

Loving our enemies isn't a platitude to be mouthed or a theory to be expounded. Jesus instructed us to practice it day by day. It's not as much of a challenge to love those who are kind and thoughtful as to love those who are rude and mean. Though we disapprove of their behavior, we are even called to love those who commit crimes and have destructive tendencies.

It's not particularly difficult to tiptoe beside a sleeping child's bed and quietly say, "I love you." It's quite another matter, however, to express love for a holy terror at the mall; for that screaming, kicking child in the grocery store; or for that angry, pouting youth who looks daggers in your direction.

I figure I made my sister the sweet, wonderful person she is today. I gave her concrete opportunities to love somebody who teased, pestered, taunted, and otherwise made her life miserable. I was kind of a pint-sized enemy under the same roof. She should be eternally grateful that I helped her grow spiritually more than all the sermons she ever heard and all the Bible studies she ever took. I expect I'll be getting a thank-you card any day now.

# —22—

## REALLY NOW, HOW DID GOD MAKE THE FIRST PEOPLE?

Some things are too rich with meaning to be explained in ordinary terms. Scientific methodology and mathematical precision fall far short of adequately expressing the deepest spiritual realities. God's act of Creation is most certainly one of these profound events. The writers of the book of Genesis understood this well, and in those first few chapters used lilting, poetic language to convey their message. "Darkness was upon the face of the deep; and the Spirit of God was moving over the face of the waters" (Genesis 1:2 RSV).

Picture in your mind how these Hebrew creation stories were passed on from generation to generation. The old village storyteller gathered the children and youth to his or her knee. As night descended, they tightly clustered around the dying flames and glowing embers of a campfire. Tales from days of yore flowed from the great storyteller's soul. Young persons sat enthralled by the dancing flames and the eloquent words. "In the beginning God created. . . ."

Had God chosen to wait until the twentieth or twenty-first centuries to create human life, it might have happened something like this: In the beginning God went shopping. The Creator made a complete list of ingredients, including sketch pad, pencils, lots of Elmer's glue, and rolls and rolls of duct tape. Then it was off to the nearest mall. In the paint department, God carefully studied the different colors, finally selecting reddish bronze, vibrant yellow, various tints of white, several shades of brown, and resplendent black. Thank goodness, God decided against purple and green.

The pieces, however, simply wouldn't fit together correctly. Discouraged, God sat down beside a pure, swiftly flowing stream to decide what to do next. Bending over to play in the moist dirt, God formed a lump into an interesting and pleasing shape. "Aha!" thought God, "I'll make my own model from the earth itself." So God lovingly crafted a human form. As a glorious sunset slipped away into the dusk, God breathed into that mass of clay the very breath of life. And God saw that it was good.

The act of creating is such delight, it's a shame we've had so many heated arguments over the details of how God brought forth life. The debates have turned our thoughts away from what truly matters: that it was God, and God alone, who fashioned us.

Does it matter whether an artist receives a sudden flash of insight and sees the entire painting in an instant, or whether the vision of the picture slowly unfolds as the ink spreads across the canvas? Are not the inner truth and beauty of the finished work what bless the viewer and are of lasting value?

Suppose a composer writes music as Handel did *Messiah* in a few short days, apparently hearing whole movements in short bursts of creativity. Yet another songwriter may labor for years or even decades over a single musical score, paying attention to every minute detail. Is one approach somehow better than the other? Or does "the proof of the pudding" occur when the notes are actually played and sung, causing the listeners' spirits to soar on high from the wonder of it all?

The question of creationism versus evolutionism may well remain until there is but one human left on the face of the planet. Some issues, and this seems to be one, produce more heat than they generate light. Perhaps the best we can do is agree to disagree agreeably.

But back to the original question. How exactly did God make the first people? No one knows for certain. There weren't any television crews present as God worked, no video camcorders, no newspaper reporters. What we do know, however, is that God's best work was done on us, birthing us in the divine image and making us partners in creation.

Instead of continuing the debate, wouldn't it be better for God's children to hush their mouths, join hands, and shout "Hallelujah"?

# —23—

## WHY DID MY GRANDPA HAVE TO SUFFER?

Dear Diary,

Why did my grandpa have to suffer so much and for so long? He was a really neat old guy. He was kind, loved everybody, and worked hard his whole life. When I was little, he'd hold me on his lap and tell me stories about his boyhood. I don't know, maybe it wasn't all completely true; but it was sure interesting.

It doesn't seem fair. He was always doing nice things for other people. He took us grandkids on backpacking trips and picnics. He taught me how to fish, including the rule that you clean whatever you catch. Yuk! He liked telling jokes, and though he repeated some of them dozens of times, I laughed at every one because he enjoyed it so much.

My grandpa had some special talents. He could "blow up" his arm muscle. He'd roll up his sleeve, put his thumb to his mouth, and blow for all he was worth. Suddenly his upper arm looked like it had an orange in it. I used to stand in front of a mirror and try it myself. Nothing ever happened.

He made great sourdough pancakes in animal shapes. He could create any animal we wanted: a deer with funny antlers, eagles soaring on the wind, rabbits with long ears and fuzzy tails, whales spouting water. He was an artist with the electric griddle. He made willow whistles and other wooden toys. I didn't think there was anything Grandpa couldn't do.

I wasn't very old when he got sick, but I could tell when he was hurting. He never complained. He'd become very quiet, which wasn't like him at all. When I'd look in his eyes, they weren't twinkling like they usually did. I sure do miss him.

Dear Diary,

I don't like to hurt. I'm no crybaby, but I don't enjoy smashing my thumb, taking a sliver out of my finger with a needle, or even getting a paper cut. Having the flu is also a bummer. I've learned something, though, from being around my grandpa. It's almost easier to have the pain yourself than to watch somebody you love suffer. I'd rather have had the flu a thousand times than to see Grandpa hurt so much.

Dear Diary,

In my Bible study class, we discussed how Jesus suffered for us. He understood that feeling good isn't nearly as important as being good. Having a healthy personality and being a whole person are what really count. By his suffering, Jesus set us free to be the best we can be. It doesn't mean everything from now on will be easy for us. We'll still get sick, have pain, and eventually die. But Jesus' suffering helps us make sense of our pain and sorrow and gives us the strength to keep going.

Dear Diary,

As long as even one other person in the world suffers, I suffer, too. I came up with this idea all by myself. Pretty good, huh? It's probably not unique, but it seems kind of profound to me.

Dear Diary,

I talked to my pastor yesterday and she was very helpful. She told me nobody knows exactly why people suffer; and that wise persons have been trying to figure it out since the beginning of time. Then she said, "I don't know why your grandpa suffered, but I'm certain God wasn't punishing him for anything he did wrong. God was not trying to teach your grandpa a lesson. God is always kind and loving."

We talked about how every living thing in the universe eventually dies. It's natural and the way things are. Suffering is often part of the process. She reminded me that we may cause some of our own problems by mistakes we make, by not taking proper care of our bodies and minds, or by not having quite enough knowledge about something. Entire societies can be at fault by polluting the environment, following unjust economic practices, allowing prejudices to go unchecked, or spending billions of dollars preparing for war. Visiting with her gave me some great insights. Thanks!

Dear Diary,

My favorite Bible verse right now is Romans 8:39. "[Nothing] will be able to separate us from the love of God in Christ Jesus our Lord" (NRSV). Even though my grandpa suffered, God was always with him and never stopped loving him.

Dear Diary,

I'm going to be okay. I'll probably be sad for awhile, but I think that's normal. When I'm feeling better, I plan to write down as many of Grandpa's jokes as I can remember, practice making animal-shaped pancakes, and work on building up my arm muscle so I can "blow" it up like he did.

## —24—

# WHAT CHURCH DOES GOD GO TO?

In my writing desk, my favorite drawer doesn't hold paper, pencils, and erasers; or a clipboard, dictionary, and thesaurus. It's crammed full of interesting toys: a little wooden popgun, a bag of marbles, a small plastic bear with soap for blowing bubbles, and a top that hums while it spins. Of all the items, though, what I treasure most is my collection of kaleidoscopes. None of them is fancy or expensive, yet each is a special friend. When I squint with one eye through the peek hole, a world of beauty miraculously appears. Even on a cloudy gray day, my kaleidoscopes do a joyful jig for me. They may be "only" children's toys, but they lift my spirits and give me hours of pleasure. They're really quite simple devices: a tube with an eye piece on one end and loose bits of brightly colored glass at the opposite end. Of course, there must be an adequate light source for illumination.

I think of the many different religions, denominations, and sects as having a potentially wonderful kaleidoscopic effect. When Jesus, the Light of the World, shines in and through them all, they create a brilliant mosaic of love; a rich variety of theology and worship; and marvelously diverse ways of being in mission. At its highest and best, the assortment of different denominations is a joy to God and a blessing for humanity.

With so many possibilities, it's no wonder children ask "What church does God go to?" The obvious answer is: all of them. God doesn't simply show up a few minutes early on Sunday morning, then head for the door right after the postlude in order to be first in the brunch line at a restaurant. The Spirit of God lives and moves within the church, broods over it, and is constantly at work in every local congregation, seven days a week, 365 days a year.

The fact that God's grace and power are active in every gathering of the saints should not be taken to mean that God completely approves of all their beliefs and practices. God is surely disappointed when religious groups quarrel among themselves over who is the biggest, the worthiest, or which one God loves the most. God is saddened when churches plead for money and then spend it exclusively on themselves. God is wearied when congregations ignore the cries of the hungry and the pleas of the homeless, and when churches keep silent in the presence of terrible injustices.

God has brought into the church people who are human, prone to making mistakes, and hesitant to risk their wealth and reputations in following where the Spirit leads. Nevertheless, God is faithful and continues to lovingly discipline, inspire, and encourage this assemblage of imperfect people. God's ultimate goal is to bring forth a community of wise, energetic, and compassionate persons who with integrity and constancy will offer Christ's healing to a broken, troubled world.

It pleases God when the various churches work side by side, putting their hands to the same plow and pulling together, freely sharing their resources and gladly uniting in service. It assuredly delights the Almighty to see such cooperation.

That which churches hold in common is far more significant than that which divides them. At first the differences may appear insurmountable; yet from the perspective of eternity, the potential for unity is clearly visible. What does it matter whether clergy are called priests, pastors, deacons, elders, or ministers if God's forgiving love is authentically proclaimed?

If everyone in the church is truly a member of the family of God, isn't the specific method by which he or she was baptized incidental? The amount of water applied through sprinkling, pouring, or immersion has nothing to do with the amount of God's grace bestowed. The day of the week set aside for worship and the place of meeting are merely matters of convenience and habit. God asks only that we worship in spirit and in truth.

Each religious group, denominations, and congregation has its own unique history and special gifts. Like the colored pieces in a kaleidoscope, they can be arranged and rearranged by God to give a waiting world visions of peace, glimpses of beauty, and rays of hope.

## —25—

# WHO SAYS IT'S MORE BLESSED TO GIVE THAN TO RECEIVE?

The doorbell rang once. I put down my evening newspaper, walked over and opened the door. No one was there. "I'm sure I heard the bell," I muttered to myself. I was about to turn back to my paper when I glanced down. On the top step was a delightful little bouquet in a homemade basket of green construction paper. It was filled with a profusion of spring flowers: fragrant lilacs, cheerful daisies, a couple of sweet buttercups, and heaps upon heaps of dandelions.

I wondered who had left it and what the occasion was. Then I remembered. This was the first day of May. Apparently, the neighborhood children were carrying on the ancient tradition of anonymously giving May baskets. What a wonderful surprise! Thoughtful young persons brought me a gift, then "rang and ran" before I could see who they were or offer them a word of thanks.

What a refreshing practice in a time when giving is mostly done with the expectation of a return, and one of equal if not greater value than the original investment! The giver usually wants credit for his or her generosity, at least a kind word or a pat on the back. Cash would be even better. There's nothing wrong with wanting that, except once in a while it's good to give for no particular reason; to do a kindness with no ulterior motives, with no hidden agendas or subtle messages; to spend oneself simply for the joy of giving. Our neighbor kids gave "just 'cuz" they wanted to give.

Children and youth may think this is all part of a grand parental conspiracy, a trick their elders play to get them to do their chores or to give rebates on their allowances. Parents may at times abuse and overuse the phrase, but its origins are solidly in the biblical tradition. In Acts 20:35 Paul asks us to remember ". . . the words of the Lord Jesus, for he himself said, 'It is more blessed to give than to receive' " (NRSV). That's the gospel! It's true through and through. Giving does bring abundant joy to the giver.

Reflecting on my own childhood, I have far clearer recollections of the gifts I gave than of those I received. Yes, I do remember the electric train I got when I was eight; and the binoculars I just had to have when I was eleven. But the memories fresh in my brain to this day are of gifts I made myself. The potholders may have been lumpy, the bookends uneven, and the mahogany coffee table I made in high school shop didn't have a square corner. But they were labors of love. And when I had my very first job, I bought my parents a shiny toaster—a four-slicer. I almost burst with pride! It was the most I'd ever spent on anybody, and this was my own hard-earned money.

When it comes to the importance of giving, parents can say to their children with complete integrity, "this is for your own good." In fact, daily lessons in giving should be offered to folks from one year of age to a hundred since it seems to go against our natural inclinations. Children know intuitively how to clench their fists, hold on tightly, and yell "Mine!" But they can also be taught the joy of letting go, the pleasure of opening their hands to give away what they have, and the blessedness of releasing the love within their souls.

People of all ages can experience the satisfaction of taking the initiative in giving. Too often we wait for other persons to reach toward us, while they stand and wait for us to make the first move. And so we pass each other in the night, remaining isolated and lonely. It need not be that way if we follow the example of One who risked everything to give, to touch, and to serve.

Gracious givers know the importance of receiving, of allowing others to give to them. In reality, giving and receiving are two sides of the same coin. Those who gladly give are usually among those who know how to humbly receive. While giving is at the apex of our human nature, the ability to receive is a precious gift, too. By opening ourselves to accept not only the gift but the heart of the giver as well, we make a lasting bequest.

## WHO SAYS IT'S MORE BLESSED TO GIVE THAN TO RECEIVE?

God's nature is to give and give and give again. God is constantly bringing forth new life and revealing beauty; eternally offering love without reservation or condition. And marvel of marvels, we are created in God's image. When we fulfill our highest purpose, we, too, give freely and never count the cost.

Who says it's more blessed to give than to receive? God's Son, that's who. It's not a trick or a subtle form of manipulation. It is by giving that we are set free to discover our truest nature. Therefore, choose the way of giving. It is the path to life's greatest joy.

# —26—

## WHY DID GOD MAKE DIFFERENT COLORS OF SKIN?

God made different colors of skin because God's an artist. Just as one color isn't adequate to create a masterpiece, one pigment cannot do justice to the beauty of the human race. Therefore, God chose a wonderful variety of colors, textures, sizes, and shapes when creating people. It should be obvious by this point in history that God enjoys dreaming up new things and creating as much diversity as possible. God is also a bit of an imp with humorous and whimsical qualities. The divine being is certainly not an old fuddy-duddy. Imagine how boring it would be if God used nothing but shades of gray when making people's skin. God is innovative, inventive, and enjoys pulling off an occasional surprise. So be on your toes.

How else can you explain a tiny hairless animal that fits in a teacup with room to spare, and a huge shaggy critter weighing hundreds of pounds, both being called dogs? I'll bet watching them has given God many a good-natured chuckle. Or what do you suppose the littlest kitten in our family would think if she came face to face with her cousin, a five hundred-pound tiger, in the jungles of India? I just hope she wouldn't come looking for me to protect her.

God loves variety. A rainbow wouldn't be such an arresting sight if it was all of one hue, no matter how bright. Autumn would lose its crowning glory if there were only evergreen trees. There'd be no golden and crimson leaves to run through, to pile up and jump in.

Personally, I'd love it if classical had a corner on the music market; but what about those folks who like rock, country and western, rap, soul, rhythm and blues, jazz, and the other forms of musical expression? They'd be sad indeed.

What would come out of the oven if sugar were the only ingredient you had in your kitchen cupboard? You'd soon get so tired of sweets you'd yearn for a pinch of salt, for a squirt of catsup, or maybe for a peanut butter sandwich. I frequently have cravings for frozen yogurt and ice cream; but if the grocery store carried nothing but vanilla, I'd get perturbed. I like to try different flavors, from Cookies 'n Cream to Peach Cobbler to Blackberry Ripple.

God must think that variety and diversity are good for humans, too. They do exert a positive influence on us, encouraging us to stay alert, stimulating us to learn and to grow. The diverse opinions people hold make us use our intelligence as we try to sort out what we ourselves believe. The wide variations in human language assist us in becoming integral parts of the world community. When we learn to communicate in languages other than our native tongue, we expand our understanding of nations and traditions and come to appreciate the rich assortment of cultures.

What a blessing it is to interact with people of different ages. We need to be together across those imaginary lines separating the generations. Generation gaps are meant to be bridged. Older persons very much enjoy the energy and enthusiasm of children. Youth need the wisdom that comes from those with years of experience. Infants require the complete care of a parent or parents. Babies, though totally dependent upon adults, give precious gifts without saying a word. They produce in the rest of us feelings of awe at God's gift of life, a love that knows no bounds, and a lively hope for the future.

In spite of the fact that God loves variety, however, we humans are sometimes afraid of differences, suspicious of what we don't know and can't explain, and hesitant to approach anything unfamiliar or accept anything new. The records of our intolerance, prejudice, narrow-mindedness, and bigotry are unfortunately numerous and well documented. What are actually inevitable changes in the universe may be perceived as threats by those who cling to the status quo.

But God the artist, the imp, the producer of this global variety show, wants us to be flexible, adaptable, and expansive. Rigid, stick-in-the-mud types don't know what to do with this constantly creative One, this God who has never made the skins of any two persons exactly the same shade. We are called to accept these differences as a challenge to become more tolerant, wise, and mature.

Perhaps some day soon, the entire human race will be able not only to passively accept, but also to actively celebrate the fullness of variety in this world, including raising their voices in a harmonious doxology for the wonderful differences in the colors of our skin.

## —27—

## INSTEAD OF MAKING NEW PEOPLE, WHY DOESN'T GOD JUST LET US LIVE LONGER?

In the earliest days of human life on earth, God apparently experimented with letting people live longer. The fifth chapter of Genesis lists some pretty impressive statistics relating to longevity. The first man, Adam, made it all the way to 930 years. His son Seth couldn't quite match Papa's feat and died at 912. Jared, however, lived to the ripe old age of 962. Pity poor Enoch who survived only to 365 years of age. What a wimp! Had there been a *Guinness Book of World Records* back then, Methuselah would have gotten the ink with an amazing 969 years.

Before you jump to the conclusion that this was a really neat idea, stop and think about the consequences. From a positive point of view, it's true that by age three hundred or so, you could finally catch up on your housework, letter writing, reading, and other projects. But there's a down side to living that long. Folks today complain about having to work forty or forty-five years before retiring. Well, some of those ancient people put in their nine to five every week for over nine hundred years. Think of filing that many income tax returns. And what about trying to plan and cook three meals per day for the duration? If my math is correct, it totals (are you ready for this?) 1,007,400. Pity poor Mrs. Methuselah if she had to be the chief cook and bottle washer.

Who could possibly think up that many clever ideas for birthday presents? I'll bet poor Methuselah never had a full complement of candles on his cake, either. And can you imagine family reunions? They don't make a camera lens with an angle wide enough to take a group picture of the thirty-five or more generations who'd assemble. What a chore to address the family patriarch with thirty-five "greats" before finally getting to "Grandpa"; plus Gramps probably would have dozed off by the time you reached "great" number twenty-five or twenty-six.

By far the major inconvenience of living so long was what happened to Noah. He became a parent at age five hundred. And I thought forty was pushing it. Here was an old duffer with five-hundred-year-old knees crawling on the hard floor chasing after sons Shem, Ham, and Japheth. Even worse, he subsequently had the pleasure of living with teenage boys when he was 513. At least Noah could regale them with stories about how tough things were when he was their age, if he could remember that far back.

God must have paused to remember how fresh and beautiful creation was when it all began. Maybe God reflected on how cute baby animals are and how human infants are such a pure delight. So God decided to make a slight modification in the original design and shortened our human life span. That way we could share with God the joys of seeing a new sunrise every morning; observe with our Creator the miracle of swelling buds, sprouting seeds, and daffodils in springtime; and participate in the never-ending mystery of birth. It could also be that the Eternal One wished to have relationships with greater numbers of the two-legged, upright creatures having the ability to communicate with their Creator.

Anyway, all living things must obey divinely established life cycles. Trees, whales, elephants, and giant sea turtles, for example, live much longer than humans. Most insects, cats, dogs, and flowers have considerably shorter life expectancies.

God chose to place the soul, our personality, inside a physical body that eventually wears out and dies. But don't worry. We believe that God provides something far more precious: a life in the spirit that is eternal.

Whatever number of years we're privileged to enjoy, God desires that we make the most of every one. Whether we live to be 20, 80, or 969, it's not the total number of years that counts but their quality. Have we spent our earthly days working for peace, seeking justice, loving and serving others, learning, growing, and in all things giving thanks?

When we do, God is pleased once again at the decision to create people who don't live quite so long but who pack a lot of love and life into each moment.